FUN SCIENCE EXPERIMENTS

FUN SCIENCE EXPERIMENTS WITH ART

Claudia Martin
Illustrated by Annie Wilkinson

WINDMILL BOOKS

Published in 2025 by Windmill Books,
an Imprint of Rosen Publishing
2544 Clinton St.
Buffalo, NY 14224

First published in Great Britain in 2022 by Wayland

Author: Claudia Martin
Illustrator: Annie Wilkinson
Designer: Clare Nicholas
Series Designer: Rocket Design (East Anglia) Ltd

Cataloging-in-Publication Data

Names: Martin, Claudia, author. | Wilkinson, Annie, illustrator.
Title: Fun science experiments with art / by Claudia Martin, illustrated by Annie Wilkinson.
Description: Buffalo, New York : Windmill Books, 2025. | Series: Fun science experiments | Includes glossary and index.
Identifiers: ISBN 9781538396469 (pbk.) | ISBN 9781538396476 (library bound) | ISBN 9781538396483 (ebook)
Subjects: LCSH: Art--Technique--Juvenile literature. | Science--Experiments--Juvenile literature.
Classification: LCC N7440.M37 2025 | DDC 701'.15--dc23

Printed in the United States of America

CPSIA Compliance Information: Batch #CSWM25. For Further Information contact Rosen Publishing at 1-800-237-9932

SAFETY PRECAUTIONS

We recommend adult supervision at all times while doing the experiments in this book. Always be aware that ingredients may contain allergens, so check the packaging for allergens if there is a risk of an allergic reaction. Anyone with a known allergy must avoid these.

* Wear an apron and cover surfaces.
* Tie back long hair.
* Ask an adult for help with cutting.
* Check all ingredients for allergens.
* Clear up all spills right away.

CONTENTS

Give art science a try!

When you make artwork, you experiment with materials to create exciting results. It is just like doing science experiments! That is why art is a fantastic way to learn about science.

Art involves lots of science. When you mix paint, you are experimenting with color. With paint in only the three primary colors – red, yellow, and blue – you can mix any color. The color of each paint depends on the way it reflects light. Sunlight looks white, but it is made up of all the colors of the rainbow. When sunlight shines through raindrops, the light is split into its different colors, creating a rainbow.

Light travels as waves, a bit like waves on the ocean. The color of light depends on how long its waves are. Red light has the longest waves, while violet has the shortest. Red paint looks red because it only reflects red light.

Sunlight is made up of waves of different colored light.

Making art is also a great way to learn about forces. Forces change the motion of an object. For example, a splatter painting makes use of the force of gravity, which pulls the drops of paint to the ground. Art can also help us learn about materials. Paint drips because it is a liquid. Pencils, paper, and clay are all solids with useful properties for an artist. Flakes from a pencil stick to paper, leaving a mark. Paper can be folded. Clay can be squeezed into marvelous models!

BECOME A SCIENTIST

Art is about using your imagination and trying new ideas. Not every artwork is perfect enough to be hung in a museum, but you still learn something from making it. Science is more similar than you might think. Scientists do not know the answer to everything. Instead, they use their imagination to come up with lots of questions. Then they suggest possible answers, called hypotheses. They test their hypotheses through experiments. Even famous scientists find their results are not what they were expecting, but they always learn something from the experiment.

When you try the experiments in this book, work as a team, use your imagination to predict the results, and ask yourself what would happen if you did something differently. Look for patterns in your results and discuss them with your team.

DO YOUR OWN THING

You can add your own creative ideas to all these experiments. Try dreaming up new combinations of colors and patterns. Think of your own ways to display your artwork, or turn them into gifts for family and friends.

Chromatography butterflies

Let's make a flock of paper butterflies with marvelously multicolored wings. We will use chromatography, which is a way of separating mixtures into their different parts.

You will need

- An adult to help you
- Paper coffee filters
- Felt-tip pens
- A pencil
- Cups
- Water
- Pipe cleaners
- Scissors
- String

1. Working as a team, choose a range of colored felt-tips, one for each member of the team. Don't avoid dark colors, as the results may surprise you!

2. Each team member should take one color and one coffee filter, then draw a thick ring about 1.5 inches (4 cm) wide in the center of their paper. Inside the ring, write the name of the color.

3. Fold each filter into a cone, by folding it in half, then in half again.

4. Each team member should half-fill a cup with water. Unfold your filter a little, then balance your cone on the rim of your cup, with only its pointed tip in the water. Don't let the colored rings touch the water.

5 While you wait for your art experiment to work, discuss with your team what you think is going to happen. Write down your predictions.

6 When the water has reached the edge of the filters, lay them flat to dry. Make a note of the color of each ring, then the colors you can see spreading away from it. Are you surprised by any of the colors? Why do you think some colors have traveled farther from the center than others?

7 When your papers are dry, pinch each one across the middle. Wrap a pipe cleaner around the middle, then twist its ends into antennae. Tie string around each butterfly's body so it can flutter from the ceiling with the rest of the flock.

DO YOUR OWN THING

If butterflies don't excite you, try making ruffle-necked monsters or winged dragons. Use pipe cleaners to shape two or three filter papers into wings and tails. Add extra pipe cleaners for legs and tongues.

What happened and why?

The ink in felt-tips is a mixture of different colored powders, called pigments, with a little liquid. We separated those pigments so we can see them all in our butterflies' wings.

Some pigments in our ink stick strongly to paper, so they did not move far when they were soaked in water. The other pigments dissolve easily in water, so their tiny solid specks of color mixed with the water.

As the water was soaked up by the filter paper, these colors were carried along with it. Some colors were carried farther than others because their specks of pigment are smaller and lighter.

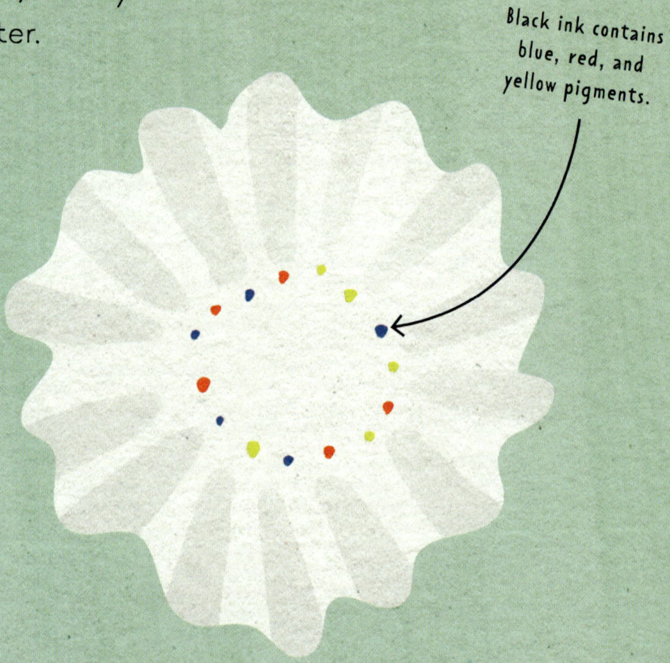

WHAT DO YOU THINK?

What do you think would happen if you used permanent markers instead of felt-tips? Why do you think we used paper coffee filters for the experiment, rather than ordinary paper or cardboard?

As you know from mixing paint, when several brightly colored paints or inks are stirred together, they turn dark. That is why we saw surprising colors when we separated black or brown inks.

The three primary colors when mixing paints and inks are blue, yellow, and red. All other colors are made from these. As a result, you probably saw that the green inks separated into blue and yellow; your purples into blue and red; and your oranges into red and yellow.

CHROMATOGRAPHY IN ACTION

Chromatography is named after the ancient Greek words for "color" (*chroma*) and "writing" (*graphein*). The method was first used to separate the different pigments in plant leaves. Today, chromatography is used in laboratories to find out if medicines are pure.

Scientists who examine crime scenes use chromatography to find out what mystery substances contain or whether the ink in a letter matches up with the ink in a suspect's pen.

Spinning splatters

As we create some super splatter art, we are going to learn about movement and forces. We will also have fun with mixing colors.

You will need

An adult to help you
Newspaper or a wipeable cloth
Apron
Paper
Pencil
Poster paints in squeezable bottles
Salad spinner (inexpensive spinners are sold in supermarkets and online)
Scissors

1 First, cover your workspace with newspaper or a wipeable cloth. Put on an apron!

2 Every member of your team will need their own circle of paper, so take turns carrying out this step. Place the salad spinner on a sheet of paper, then draw around the edge with a pencil. Cut out your paper circle, which should fit neatly inside your salad spinner.

3 Choose which member of the team will go first. They can choose their paint colors.

4 Place a circle of paper at the bottom of the salad spinner. Squeeze a few blobs of different colored paints onto the paper. You could experiment with putting all the blobs in the center or dotting them around in patterns.

5 Close the lid of the salad spinner. Turn the handle or press the top to spin the spinner! For the most dramatic results, spin it fast.

6 Open the lid to see your art. What has happened?

DO YOUR OWN THING

There are lots of fun ways to display your circular splatter artwork. If it is winter, fold them into cones, then carefully snip triangles along the edges to make colorful snowflakes. For a summer display, gather the circles in the middle with tape, then stick them to a green-painted paper towel tube to make flowers.

7 Each member of the team should take a turn at Steps 4–6.

8 Discuss your results with your team. How did the positions and colors of your paint blobs make a difference to your artwork? Display your team's art!

What happened and why?

Our paint blobs splattered and mixed because of centrifugal force. This is an effect that can be felt by someone in a car on a winding road – or by a spinning blob of paint.

Centrifugal force is an effect that causes a turning object to move outward from a center point. In this case, the center point was the middle of the salad spinner. You can feel centrifugal force when you are being driven along a winding road. When the car moves swiftly around a bend to the left, you feel yourself moving to the right.

WHAT DO YOU THINK?

What do you think would happen if you spun your salad spinner very slowly? What might be the result if you put your paint blobs only around the edges of the paper?

In fact, nothing is actually pushing you to the right! But we feel centrifugal force as a push to the right. Since your body has been traveling straight ahead, it just carries on moving straight ahead, even though the car has turned left. Your body is like a marble that has been rolled across a flat table: it carries on moving in the same direction – until it is held back by a seatbelt!

As you turned the handle of the salad spinner, the paper spun inside the container. The paint blobs tried to keep moving straight ahead, which caused them to travel outward from the center of the paper. This may have made your paint colors mix together. For example, if you used primary colors, like yellow and blue, they may have mixed together into a secondary color, such as green.

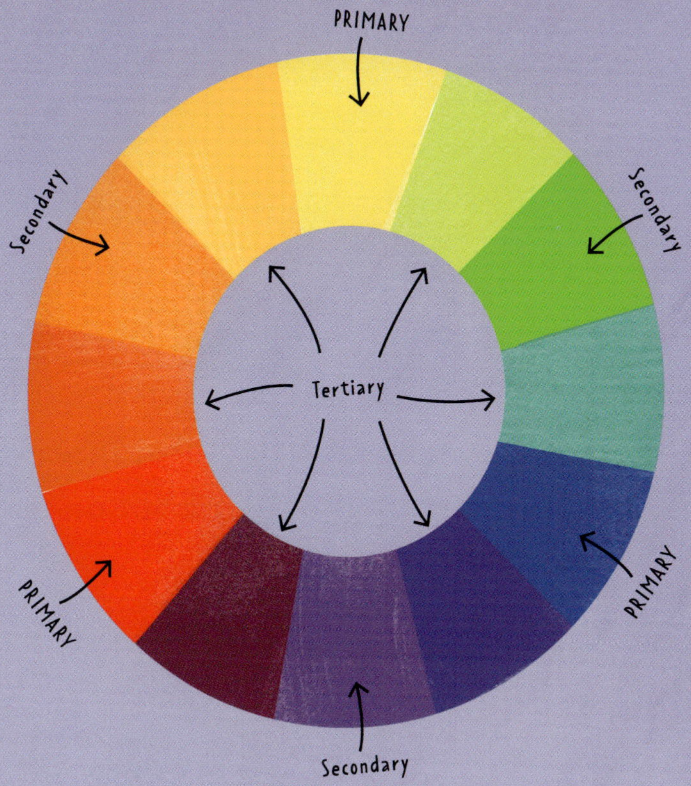

Every color of the rainbow can be made by mixing the three primary colors of paint. Mixing primary colors makes secondary colors. Mixing a primary and a secondary makes a tertiary color.

CENTRIFUGES IN ACTION

A salad spinner is a centrifuge. A centrifuge is a machine that uses centrifugal force to separate mixtures. This is possible because centrifugal force is felt most strongly by heavier objects and materials. In a laboratory, a centrifuge can separate blood or chemicals into their different parts so they can be studied.

Rainbow oobleck

We are going to find out more about the properties of liquids and solids by making oobleck! This substance gets its name from a book about an oozy slime by Dr. Seuss.

You will need

An adult to help you
9 oz. (250 g) arrowroot flour
1 cup (200 ml) water
Gel food coloring
A large bowl or dish
Measuring cup
Spoons
6 small bowls

1. Put on an apron and cover your work surface with newspaper or a plastic cloth.

2. Weigh out 9 ounces of arrowroot flour. Pour it into a large bowl.

3. Using a measuring cup, measure 1 cup of water. Add the water to the arrowroot, then stir to combine. You may find stirring difficult, as arrowroot oobleck behaves oddly even as you make it! Does the oobleck seem like a liquid or a solid when you stir with your spoon?

4. If you would like to make rainbow oobleck, divide your mixture in six small bowls. Add a drop of different gel food coloring to each one. Stir thoroughly.

5. Pour your rainbow-colored ooblecks back into the main bowl. Swirl to create rainbows and patterns. As soon as you play with your oobleck, the colors will start to mix!

6 Slap and punch your oobleck. Does it behave like a liquid or a solid? Squeeze a fistful of oobleck, then open your fingers. Does the oobleck flow from your fingers like a liquid or stay on your palm like a solid? Why do you think the oobleck is behaving differently from an ordinary solid or an ordinary liquid?

7 When you have finished playing with your oobleck, do not pour it down the sink because it will clog up the pipes. Either put it in the compost bin or throw it away with the ordinary household trash.

DO YOUR OWN THING

Make your oobleck glittery by sprinkling in biodegradable glitter. Unlike ordinary glitter, which is made of plastic, biodegradable glitter is made of natural materials, which will decompose. Avoid plastic glitter, which can be washed into oceans and eaten by fish.

What happened and why?

When you let the oobleck trickle through your fingers, it flowed like a liquid. Yet when you squeezed, slapped, or punched it, it behaved like a solid.

Oobleck is a non-Newtonian fluid. "Non-Newtonian" means that it does not follow the scientist Isaac Newton's rules about how liquids flow. Non-Newtonian fluids can behave like a solid or a liquid depending on the force applied to them. All materials are made of groups of atoms, called molecules. In a liquid, the molecules are not joined together so they move freely, allowing a liquid to flow. In a solid, the molecules are bonded to each other, giving a solid a definite shape.

In a liquid, the molecules are not joined, so a liquid can flow.

In a solid, the molecules are joined in a rigid pattern.

NON-NEWTONIAN FLUIDS IN ACTION

Another non-Newtonian fluid is toothpaste, which also changes how it behaves under pressure. Yet toothpaste behaves quite differently from oobleck! When toothpaste is put under pressure (by being squeezed out of the tube), it flows like a liquid. When it is not under pressure (just sitting on the brush), it behaves like a solid. Toothpaste contains lots of long molecules that, when at rest, link together to form a weak solid. Pressure breaks those weak links.

Our oobleck is non-Newtonian because of the arrowroot particles floating in the water. When the oobleck is not under pressure, there is a little water between each particle of arrowroot. This allows the fluid to flow, with the arrowroot carried along with the water. Yet when the arrowroot particles are squeezed together, the particles rub against each other so they do not flow easily. This makes the oobleck behave like a solid. Arrowroot oobleck even forms solid lumps if it is poured, since the particles bunch together.

Marbled paper

We are going to try a Japanese technique called *suminagashi* (meaning "floating ink") to create marbled paper. We will make use of the fact that some liquids just do not mix!

You will need

An adult to help you
Vegetable oil
Liquid food coloring
Pieces of watercolor paper around 4 x 6 inches (10 x 15 cm)
Small bowls or jars
Baking tin or large bowl (big enough to fit your paper)
Teaspoons

1 Measure 3 tablespoons of vegetable oil into a small bowl or jar. Add a few drops of food coloring. Whisk with a fork so the food coloring is spread evenly through the oil.

2 Repeat Step 1 for every color your team would like to work with. Use a different bowl for each color.

3 Pour water into your baking tin until it is about 1 inch (2.5 cm) deep.

4 Using a teaspoon, put a few drops of your colored oils onto the water. What do you notice about how the oils behave in the water? If you like, gently use a spoon to create swirls.

DO YOUR OWN THING

Make a birthday card by sticking your marbled paper onto a folded piece of cardboard. For a really dramatic design, turn your paper into a sunset scene. Use a black felt-tip pen to draw simple V-shaped birds flying across the marbled sunset sky.

5. Lay your paper on top of the water for 30 to 40 seconds.

6. Remove your paper, using your fingertips to grasp the edges, then lay it flat to dry. How would you describe the patterns on your paper? Why do you think they have formed?

7. Repeat Steps 5 and 6 as many times as you like. You will probably need to change your water after every couple of tries, since it will become too muddy to give pretty results.

8. Display your marbled paper!

What happened and why?

Our marbling technique used the fact that oil and water do not mix. This is because of a particular property of water: polarity.

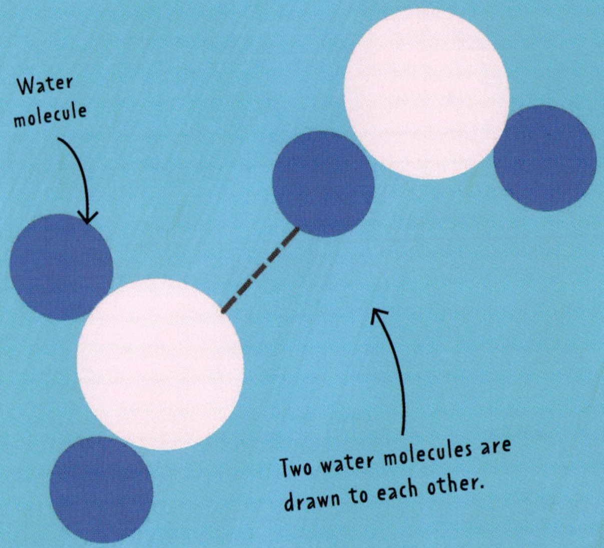

The molecules in a liquid can be polar or nonpolar. Polar liquids will mix with other polar liquids, while nonpolar liquids will only mix with nonpolar liquids. Water is polar. Its polar molecules are like little magnets, as they attract other polar molecules. Oil is nonpolar. Oil molecules are not attracted to water molecules – they are repelled (pushed away) by them. This stops the two liquids from mixing.

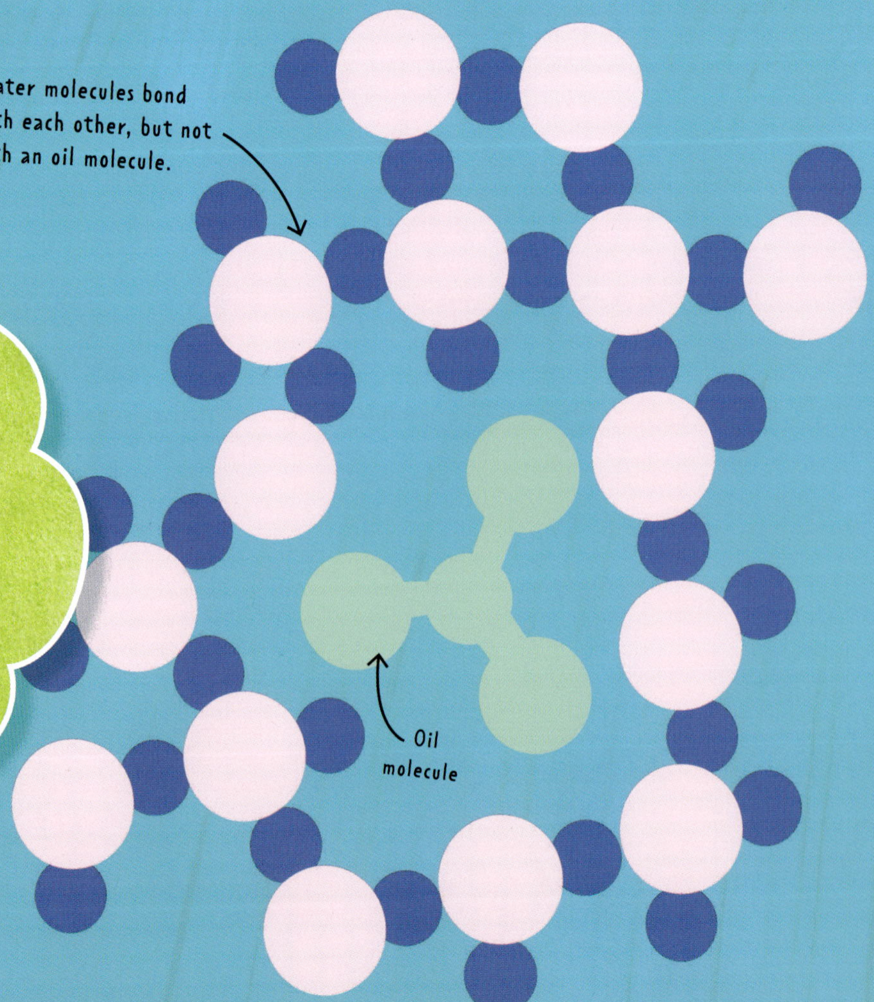

WHAT DO YOU THINK?

What would happen if you did not mix your food coloring with oil, but just dropped it right into the water?

The colored oil floated on the water surface because it is less dense than water. This means that its molecules are less tightly packed together. Anything that is less dense than water – such as a foam swimming float – will float.

When the watercolor paper was placed in the baking tin, it soaked up food coloring and water. As the paper dried, the water evaporated, turning to invisible gas in the air. The pigment in the food coloring stayed on the paper.

POLARITY IN ACTION

Since water molecules are attracted to each other, they create surface tension. This means that the molecules on the surface of water stick strongly to each other, making a surface "film." Insects such as water striders can skate across the water surface because their weight is not great enough to break this delicate film.

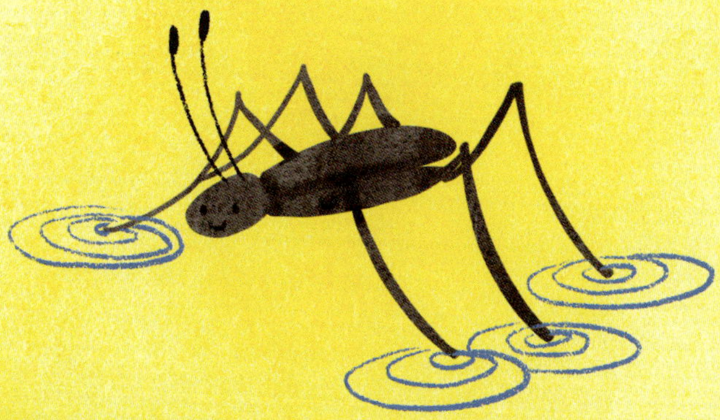

Pendulum painting

Let's create swirling, surprising modern art using a pendulum. A pendulum is an object that is hung from a point so that it can swing freely.

You will need

- An adult to help you
- Plastic tarp or trash bags
- 2 chairs or tables
- Broom or 3-foot (1-m) ruler
- Duct tape
- Paper or polystyrene cup
- String
- Poster paints
- Large sheets of paper
- Pencil
- Scissors

1. If the weather is good, this experiment could be done outside. Wherever you are working, cover the floor or ground with a plastic tarp or trash bags.

2. Working with your team, position two chairs or tables so that your broom can rest horizontally between them. Leave room between your chairs for you to swing a pendulum. When your structure is well balanced, secure the broom using duct tape.

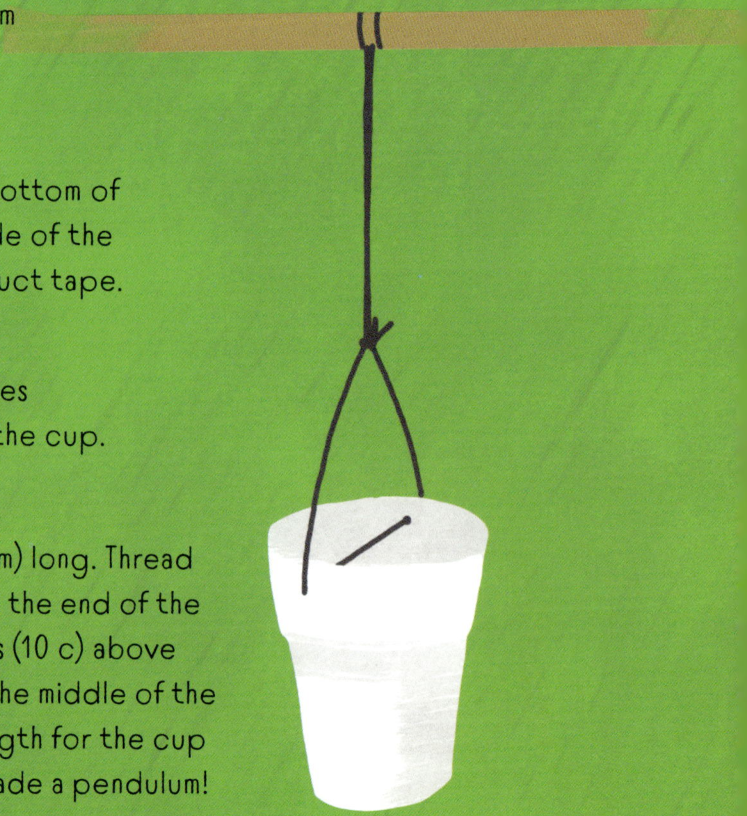

3. ! **With an adult's help**, make a hole in the bottom of your cup using a pencil. On the underside of the cup, cover the hole with a small piece of duct tape.

4. ! **Ask an adult to help** with making two holes close to the cup's rim, on either side of the cup.

5. Cut a piece of string about 30 inches (80 cm) long. Thread it through both rim holes in the cup, then tie the end of the string to the length of string, about 4 inches (10 c) above the cup. Tie the other end of the string to the middle of the broom. Make sure your string is the right length for the cup to swing freely above the floor. You have made a pendulum!

6 Place a large piece of paper beneath your pendulum.

7 Put a few squirts of paint into the cup. Remove the duct tape from the bottom of the cup, then swing your pendulum. Try swinging it forward and backward, as well as in gentle circles. What happens if you do not stop the pendulum? If the paint does not flow through the hole easily, try making the hole bigger or adding a little water to the paint.

8 When all the paint has trickled out of the cup, use a different color.

9 Repeat Steps 6–8 for every member of the team.

10 Discuss your artwork. What do the patterns tell you about the movement of a pendulum?

DO YOUR OWN THING

Try turning your artwork into a picture of a snail with a spiraling, multicolored shell. Use felt pens or paints to add the snail's head and body, complete with its antennae, or feelers.

What happened and why?

We built our pendulum from a cup and string. When our pendulum was raised and released, it moved freely backward and forward due to the force of gravity.

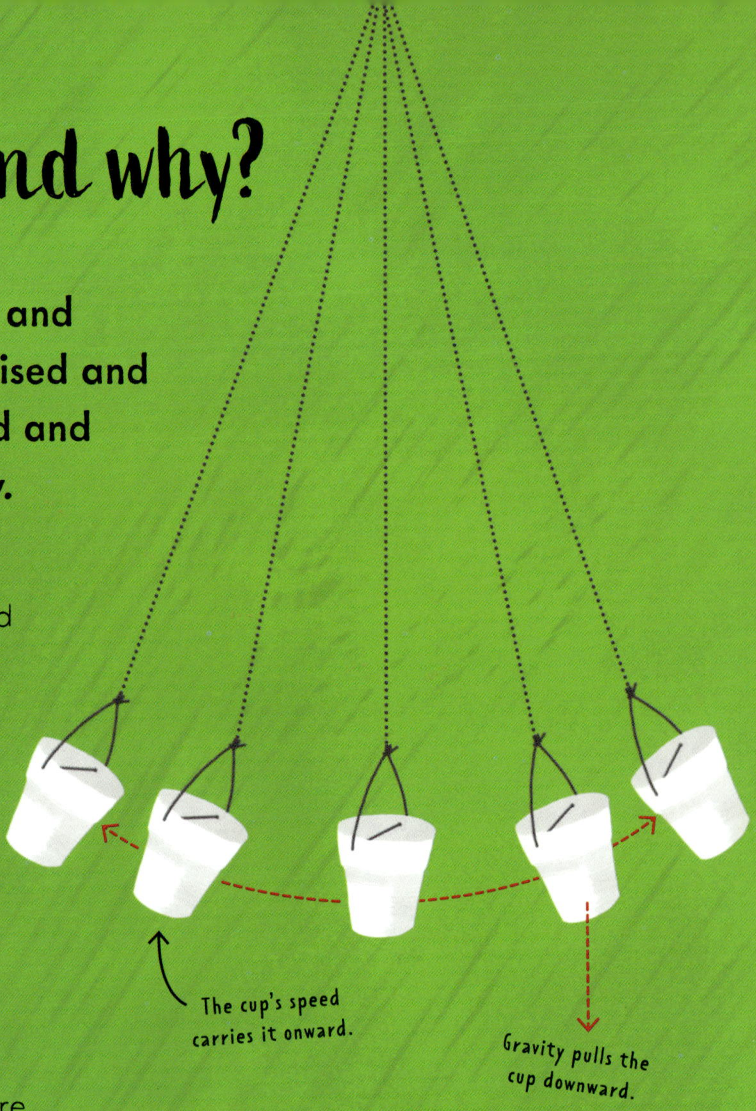

Gravity is a force that pulls all objects toward each other. Yet the larger the object, the greater the pull of its gravity. This is why we are pulled back to Earth when we jump, as Earth is much bigger than us! Since our cup was attached to a string, it could not fall to the ground. Instead, when our cup was swung, it was pulled downward by gravity until its string was vertical.

However, the cup's "fall" from its higher position gave the pendulum speed. Since there was nothing to stop its movement, the pendulum carried on moving forward. As the cup swung higher, it was working against the force of gravity, which made it slow to a stop. Then gravity pulled it back again.

WHAT DO YOU THINK?

What would happen if you swung the pendulum harder or really softly? How would your artwork change if you made the string longer or shorter?

The swinging of your pendulum continued until friction (the "rubbing" of the cup against the air) slowed it down, shortened its swings, and finally stopped it. If you experimented with changing the length of your string, you probably noticed that a pendulum with a longer string takes longer to complete each swing.

PENDULUMS IN ACTION

Japanese engineers have designed pendulums to stop skyscrapers from swaying violently during earthquakes. Engineers are placing pendulums on the upper floors of skyscrapers. As the upper floors sway to the left, the pendulums are pulled by gravity so they swing to the right. This reduces the building's sway and protects everyone inside.

Colorful copters

We will design our own little helicopters to find out more about lift. This is a force that helps to keep full-size helicopters in the air.

You will need

- An adult to help you
- Paper measuring 6 x 1.5 inches
- Pencil
- Ruler
- Scissors
- Small paper clip
- Colored pencils or felt-tip pens

1. Using a pencil and ruler, draw this pattern onto your paper. Measure out the lengths as marked, trying to be as exact as possible.

2. Cut along the solid lines only. You are making just three cuts! The dotted lines mark the folds, so try not to cut through them.

3. Folding along the dotted lines, fold C and D over each other. Fold the bottom up along the dotted line. Secure this fold with a paper clip.

4. Decorate your helicopter using colored pencils or felt-tips. You might like to use stripes or spots. Remember to decorate both sides.

5 Fold A toward you and B away from you. These are your helicopter's blades.

6 Test your copter! While holding your helicopter by the paper clip, throw it away from you, high and hard. Remember that paper clips can be sharp so take turns throwing and aiming it away from other people. How does your copter behave after you let it go? Which way is your copter spinning: clockwise or counterclockwise?

7 Now bend your copter's blades the opposite way, with A away from you and B toward you. Throw your copter again. Which way does it spin now?

8 Finally, examine how your pattern appears as your copter falls. Can you still see the different colors that you used to decorate it?

DO YOUR OWN THING

Try decorating your copter like a parrot by drawing eyes and a yellow hooked beak on the helicopter's central "body." The copter's blades can be scarlet or emerald wings, while the base of the copter is a long feathery tail.

What happened and why?

As your copter fell, the shape of its blades made it spin round and round. This spinning created a force called lift, which slowed the copter's fall to the ground.

As your copter fell, the weight of the paper clip kept the base of the copter pointing downward. Air pushed against the blades, bending them up a little. Some of that pushing force became a sideways push. The two blades were pushed in opposite directions, making your copter spin.

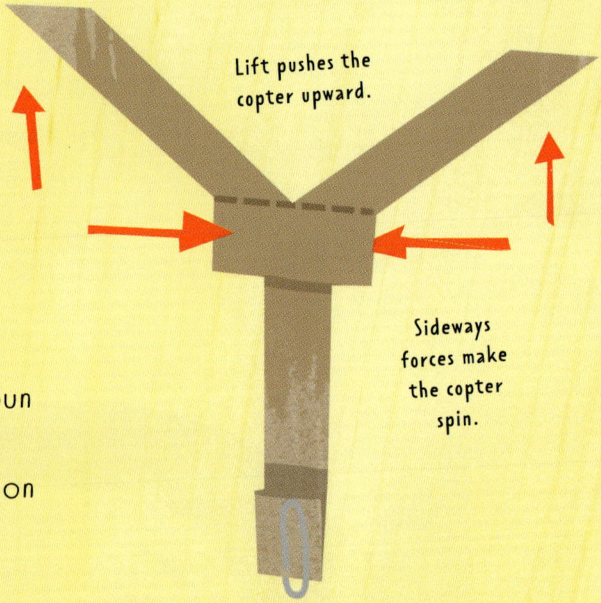

When A was folded toward you, your copter spun clockwise. When you reversed the fold, it spun counterclockwise. The spinning made the colors on your copter seem to blur together.

WHAT DO YOU THINK?

What would happen if you made the blades of your copter longer or shorter? If you used cardboard rather than light paper for your copter, would it fly for less time or more time?

Lift is created by differences in air pressure above and below an object. When the molecules in air are more tightly packed, they create higher air pressure. For your copter, the air moved more quickly over the top of the spinning blades than below them, so the air pressure above the copter was lower than under the copter. This created lift, pushing the copter up.

Since your copter has no engine, it did not actually fly upward, but lift slowed your copter's fall.

LIFT IN ACTION

The seeds of sycamore trees are shaped a little like our copters. As they fall from their tree, they spin. This creates lift, which – when helped by wind – can carry the seeds a long distance. This allows new sycamore trees to grow away from the shadow of their parent tree.

Glossary

air pressure the force exerted by air on any surface it touches

atom the smallest portion of anything that can exist on its own

biodegradable able to decay naturally in a way that is not harmful to the environment

chromatography a method of separating a mixture by passing it through a medium in which the different parts of the mixture move at different speeds

dense tightly packed with molecules

dissolve when a solid breaks up and mixes with a liquid

evaporate to turn from a liquid into a gas

film a thin surface layer

force a push or pull that can change an object's motion

gas a substance that has no fixed shape or volume, so it will expand to fill any container

ink a liquid that contains a dye or pigment

lift an upward force created by gas or liquid flowing around an object

liquid a substance that flows but has a fixed volume (takes up a certain amount of space)

molecule a group of atoms that are bonded together

pigment a colored material, often a powder, that is mixed with liquid to make ink

plastic a human-made material, often made from oil

polarity having two poles, with opposite poles attracting each other and similar poles repelling each other

primary colors the three basic colors of paint – red, yellow, and blue – that can be mixed together to make other colors

secondary colors the three colors – orange, green, and purple – that can be made by mixing two primary colors of paint

solid a substance that has a fixed shape

tertiary colors the six colors that can be made by mixing a primary color with a secondary color of paint

Further reading

BOOKS

Forces (Science in a Flash),
Georgia Amson-Bradshaw (Gareth Stevens, 2018)

Let's Make Art with Everyday Things,
Susie Brooks (Wayland, 2016)

Making with Forces (Science Makers),
Anna Claybourne (Wayland, 2018)

The Story of Paintings: A History of Art for Children,
Mick Manning and Brita Granström (Franklin Watts, 2017)

WEBSITES

Find out more about color, forces, and materials on these websites:

https://kids.britannica.com/kids/article/force/400287

https://sciencing.com/ten-different-types-forces-7459343.html

www.bbc.co.uk/bitesize/articles/zm7ntrd

www.bbc.co.uk/bitesize/topics/zw982hv/articles/z7rtng8

Index